Spot the Difference

Feet

Diyan Leake

www.heinemann.co.uk/library
Visit our website to find out more information about Heinemann Library books.

To order:
 Phone 44 (0) 1865 888066
Send a fax to 44 (0) 1865 314091
 Visit the Heinemann Bookshop at www.heinemann.co.uk/library to browse our
catalogue and order online.

First published in Great Britain by Heinemann Library,
Halley Court, Jordan Hill, Oxford OX2 8EJ, part of Harcourt
Education. Heinemann is a registered trademark of Harcourt
Education Ltd.

Editorial: Diyan Leake and Cassie Mayer
Design: Joanna Hinton-Malivoire
Picture research: Erica Martin
Production: Duncan Gilbert

Originated by Chroma Graphics (Overseas) Pte Ltd
Printed and bound in China by South China Printing Co. Ltd

ISBN 978 0 4311 9137 9

11 10 09 08 07
10 9 8 7 6 5 4 3 2 1

British Library Cataloguing in Publication Data
Leake, Diyan
Feet. - (Spot the difference)
1. Foot - Juvenile literature 2. Animals - Juvenile
literature
I. Title
591.4'79

Acknowledgements
The publishers would like to thank the following for permission
to reproduce photographs: Alamy/Juniors Bildarchiv p. **8**;
Animal Photography pp. **9**, **23** top; Digital Vision p. **18**,
back cover; FLPA/Frans Lanting/Minden Pictures pp. **14**,
22; FLPA/Martin B Withers p. **11**; Jupiter Images/Workbook
stock/Natural Moments Photography Ltd p. **20**; Nature
Picture Llibrary pp. **4** (Tony Heald), **5** (Staffan Widstrand),
6 (Simon King), **7** (Carol Walker), **10** (Tony Heald), **12**
(Elliott Bignell), **16** (Pete Oxford), **22** (Pete Oxford); NHPA/
Kevin Schafer pp. **15**, **23** middle; Photolibrary/Animals
Animals/Earth Scenes p. **17**; Photolibrary/Imagestate Ltd
p. **21**; Photolibrary/Michael Fogden pp. **13**, **23** bottom;
Photolibrary/Satyendra K. Tiwari p. **19**.

Cover photograph of the feet of a blue-footed booby
reproduced with permission of Getty Image/National
Geographic/Timothy Laman.

Every effort has been made to contact copyright holders
of any material reproduced in this book. Any omissions will
be rectified in subsequent printings if notice is given to the
publishers.

Contents

What are feet?

Feet are part of an animal's body.

Feet are usually on the end of an
animal's legs.

Why do animals have feet?

Animals use their feet to stand on.

Animals use their feet to move.

Different feet

Feet come in many shapes and sizes.

This is a dog.
It has furry feet.

This is an elephant.
It has big, round feet.

This is a bird.

It has small, thin feet.

Can you spot the difference?

This is a snail.
It has one foot.

This is a frog.
It has four webbed feet.

Amazing feet

This is a gecko.
It has sticky feet.

This is a sloth.
It has feet like hooks.

blue-footed booby

This is a bird.
It has blue feet.

This is a lizard.

It can run across water.

Can you spot the difference?

This is an ape.

It can climb with its feet.

This is a butterfly.

It can taste things with its feet.

Your feet

People have feet, too.

People use their feet to move.
People are like other animals.

Can you remember?

Which animal has sticky feet?
Which animal has webbed feet?

Picture glossary

 **furry** lots of soft hair

 **hook** something bent that can be used to hang on to things

 **webbed** skin that joins its toes together

Index

Notes for parents and teachers

Before reading

Talk to the children about their feet. Tell them to take off their socks and shoes and help them to find their toes, heel, sole, ankle, big toe, and toe nails. Ask them to think about animals' feet. Do all animals have toes? Do all animals have nails?

After reading

• Place some plastic sheeting on the floor and then mix four different colours of washable paint and put each in a shallow tray. Tell the children to choose a colour and then, in bare feet, to step in to the tray of paint and to walk carefully along the wallpaper, making painty footprints. When dry, display the footprints on the wall.

• Draw the foot shapes of some different animals and ask the children to guess which animal made the prints, such as round prints from an elephant, arrow prints from a bird, a pad and four toe prints from a dog, or flat, webbed triangular prints from a duck.

• Help the children learn the tongue-twister: "Moses supposes his toeses are roses, but Moses supposes erroneously. For nobody's toeses are posies of roses as Moses supposes his toeses to be!"